HOSTAGE NEGOTIATORS

Katie Kawa

New York

Published in 2016 by The Rosen Publishing Group, Inc.
29 East 21st Street, New York, NY 10010

First Edition

Editor: Katherine Kawa
Book Design: Mickey Harmon

Photo Credits: Cover, p. 22 (woman) Straight 8 Photography/Shutterstock.com; cover (background) Wally Stemberger/Shutterstock.com; cover, pp. 1, 3, 4, 6, 8, 10, 12–13, 14, 16, 18, 20, 22–24 (gray and yellow textures) siro46/Shutterstock.com; p. 5 JOEL NITO/Stringer/AFP/Getty Images; p. 7 courtesy of the United States Air Force; p. 9 pio3/Shutterstock.com; p. 11 Leonard Zhukovsky/Shutterstock.com; p. 12 courtesy of the Federal Bureau of Investigation; p. 13 (graphic) Tarapong Siri/Shutterstock.com; p. 15 Jon L. Hendricks/AP Images; p. 17 John Roman Images/Shutterstock.com; p. 18 (policeman) RDaniel/Shutterstock.com; p. 19 Oleg Zabielin/Shutterstock.com; p. 21 Bloomberg/Contributor/Getty Images.

Cataloging-in-Publication Data

Kawa, Katie.
Hostage negotiators / by Katie Kawa.
p. cm. — (Careers for heroes)
Includes index.
ISBN 978-1-5081-4379-6 (pbk.)
ISBN 978-1-5081-4380-2 (6-pack)
ISBN 978-1-5081-4381-9 (library binding)
1. Hostages — Juvenile literature. 2. Rescues — Juvenile literature. 3. United States. — Federal Bureau of Investigation. — Hostage Rescue Team — Juvenile literature. I. Kawa, Katie. II. Title.
HV6571.K39 2016
363.2'3—d23

Manufactured in the United States of America

CPSIA Compliance Information: Batch #BW16PK: For Further Information contact Rosen Publishing, New York, New York at 1-800-237-9932

CONTENTS

Staying Calm in a Crisis   4

Two Names, One Job   6

Starting in New York   8

Part of a Team   10

Buying Time   12

Other Objectives   14

Special Skills   16

Experience Is Important   18

A Crisis in New Hampshire   20

Do You Have What It Takes?   22

Glossary   23

Index   24

Websites   24

STAYING CALM IN A CRISIS

In times of crisis, or danger, it's important to stay calm and keep others calm, too. This ability is especially important for hostage negotiators. They're men and women trained to **respond** to dangerous, or unsafe, **situations** involving hostages. A hostage is a person who's held against their will by someone who plans to trade them for something else.

Negotiators are people who formally discuss things in order to reach an agreement. Hostage negotiators try to reach an agreement with people who take hostages. It's their job to do everything they can to get the hostages out of harm's way.

FAST FACT!

Around 80 **percent** of hostage situations end without anyone getting injured, or hurt.

In a hostage situation, it's the negotiator's job to talk to the captor, or the person who's holding people hostage. Negotiators are trained to calmly handle these scary situations.

TWO NAMES, ONE JOB

Not all dangerous situations that call for negotiators are hostage situations. In fact, as of 2013, only 4 percent of all situations involving police negotiators were hostage situations.

What made up the other 96 percent? These situations involved people who took others against their will or were threatening to harm themselves without asking for anything from the police. These situations are called crisis situations. Because of this, some **law enforcement agencies**, such as the Federal Bureau of Investigation (FBI), call their negotiators—including those who deal with hostages—"crisis negotiators." No matter what the negotiators are called, they all use the same skills to control dangerous situations.

FAST FACT!

A person who's held against their will without their captor asking for anything in return is called a "victim" rather than a "hostage."

One of the most famous crisis negotiation units, or teams, in the world is the FBI's Crisis Negotiation Unit (CNU).

STARTING IN NEW YORK

Hostage negotiators are a very important part of police forces around the world. However, the first team created to deal specifically with hostage situations wasn't formed until 1973. Before that time, police officers responded with force to situations that are now often **resolved** by negotiation.

In 1973, the New York City Police Department created the first team to deal with possible hostage situations. It was named the Hostage Negotiation Team (HNT). The HNT used **communication** skills instead of immediate force. Today, the HNT is still considered one of the best hostage negotiation teams in the world.

FAST FACT!

The HNT was formed because many hostage situations ended with people getting hurt, and leaders wanted to find another, safer way to resolve these crises.

The first brave members of the HNT forever changed the way people respond to hostage situations.

PART OF A TEAM

Hostage negotiators most often work in teams of brave men and women who work well with others. The negotiator is the person who talks directly to the person who's taken hostages. Above the negotiator is a commander.

It's important that the negotiator and commander are two different people. A negotiator can buy more time when talking to someone who's taken hostages by telling them they need to talk to their commander before making any decisions. This can't happen if the negotiator is working alone.

FAST FACT!

Sometimes a hostage negotiator gets stuck and can't find the right thing to say to the person who's taken hostages. This is why it's good to have another negotiator on the scene, so the two can help each other.

Working as part of a team takes away some of the **stress** hostage negotiators are under when they're on the job. This helps them stay calm and clearheaded while dealing with dangerous people.

BUYING TIME

A hostage negotiator must be skilled in using different **tactics** to meet their most important objectives, or goals, at the scene of a dangerous situation. The hostage negotiator's main goal is to buy time. The longer a hostage or crisis situation lasts, the more likely it is to end peacefully.

One way hostage negotiators can buy time is by asking the captor to be specific about their demands. It's also important for the hostage negotiator to ask open-ended questions. These are questions that call for more than just a "yes" or "no" answer.

FAST FACT!

In some cases, hostages begin to care for their captors after spending a long time with them. This is called Stockholm Syndrome. Hostage negotiators need to be able to recognize this in case the hostages try to help their captors.

Why is buying time so important?

1 More police officers can arrive on the scene.

2 It allows officers at the scene to learn as much as possible about the place where the hostages are being kept and about the captor.

3 As more time passes, captors are more likely to calm down and begin to think more clearly.

4 More time allows the negotiator to build a rapport, or sense of understanding, with the person who took the hostages.

5 The captor could begin to see the hostages as people and not just as things to trade if they spend more time with the hostages. This would make them less likely to hurt the hostages.

The ability to buy time is one of a hostage negotiator's most important skills. Buying time in a hostage or other crisis situation can save lives!

OTHER OBJECTIVES

While the most important thing a hostage negotiator should be able to do is buy time, they also have other objectives to meet when dealing with a crisis situation. They need to get any sick or injured hostages out of the situation. They also need to get hostages food and water.

Another important objective is to keep things calm. A hostage negotiator should be a person who can stay calm under large amounts of stress. This allows them to keep the person they're talking to as calm as possible, which makes for a safer situation for the hostages.

FAST FACT!

Hostage negotiators should never argue with the person they're talking to. It's not always easy, and that's why only certain types of people make good hostage negotiators.

Hostage negotiators are often able to keep dangerous situations calm and controlled long enough to get hostages out without any injuries.

SPECIAL SKILLS

Hostage negotiation isn't the right job for everyone. It calls for a very specific set of skills and **traits** that generally can't be taught. The most important characteristic of a good hostage negotiator is self-control. A hostage negotiator needs to be able to control their feelings in even the most stressful situations.

Someone who wants to be a hostage negotiator should also have strong communication skills. Good listening skills help hostage negotiators because they spend much of their time listening to the demands of captors. Also, hostage negotiators must be able to work well with the others on their team.

FAST FACT!

Hostage negotiators must be quick thinkers in order to **react** in the best possible way to sudden changes in crisis situations.

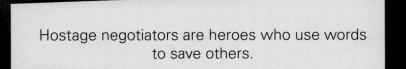

Hostage negotiators are heroes who use words to save others.

EXPERIENCE IS IMPORTANT

If you think you have the skills needed to be a good hostage negotiator, the next step is to gain **experience** in law enforcement. Hostage negotiators generally work as police or FBI officers for some time first as they learn how to deal with crisis situations.

People who want to become hostage negotiators also go through training before starting on this new career path. The training involves studying how past crises were handled. It also involves role-playing, or acting as if a real crisis situation is taking place, in order to learn what to do in a realistic setting.

FAST FACT!

The FBI and other law enforcement agencies offer training programs that negotiators must take throughout their career in order to keep their skills sharp.

POLICE

Serving in the military is also a good way to gain experience dealing with crisis situations.

A CRISIS IN NEW HAMPSHIRE

In 2007, hostage negotiators in Rochester, New Hampshire, put their training to lifesaving use when a man took hostages inside Hillary Clinton's presidential campaign office. He also claimed to have a **bomb** strapped to his chest.

Through successful negotiation tactics, all the hostages were eventually released without any harm coming to them. The man who took the hostages, Lee Eisenberg, also surrendered, or gave himself up to the police. The bomb turned out to be **road flares** held together with duct tape.

FAST FACT!

During many crisis situations such as this one, roads, businesses, and schools are often shut down. The people in nearby buildings are told to leave for their own safety.

After the crisis ended, Clinton praised the bravery of the heroic hostage negotiators who helped control what could have been a deadly crisis.

DO YOU HAVE WHAT IT TAKES?

Hostage negotiators are heroes who use a very special set of skills to save lives. With a calm, upbeat attitude and strong communication skills, they can help scary situations end peacefully.

It takes a lot of experience and training to become a hostage negotiator. It also takes skills and traits not every person has. If you think you have what it takes to become a heroic hostage negotiator, keep sharpening those skills. Practice being a good listener, and notice how you handle stressful situations. It's never too early to start training for this lifesaving career!

GLOSSARY

bomb: A device made to explode under certain conditions in order to hurt people or destroy property.

communication: The use of words, sounds, signs, or behaviors to convey ideas, thoughts, and feelings.

experience: The length of time someone has been doing a job.

law enforcement agency: A government department that is formed with the purpose of making sure laws are followed.

percent: A part of a whole. One percent is one part in a hundred.

react: To behave in a certain way when something happens.

resolve: To find an answer or solution to something.

respond: To do something as a reaction to something that has happened.

road flare: An object that produces bright light in order to warn people of obstacles on roads.

situation: All the facts, conditions, and events that affect someone or something in a certain time and place.

stress: Something that causes strong feelings of worry.

tactic: An action that is planned and used to reach a certain goal.

trait: A quality that makes one person or thing different from another.

INDEX

C
captor, 5, 6, 12, 13, 16
CNU, 7
commander, 10
communication, 8, 16, 22
crisis situation, 6, 12, 13, 14,
　　　16, 18, 19, 20

E
experience, 18, 19, 22

F
FBI, 6, 7, 18

H
HNT, 8, 9
hostages, 4, 6, 10, 12, 13, 14,
　　　15, 20

L
listening, 16, 22

M
military, 19

N
New York City Police
　　　Department, 8

O
objectives, 12, 14

P
police, 6, 8, 13, 18, 20

S
self-control, 16
skills, 6, 8, 13, 16, 18, 22
Stockholm Syndrome, 12
stress, 11, 14, 16, 22

T
tactics, 12, 20
teams, 7, 8, 10, 11, 16
training, 18, 20, 22
traits, 16, 22

V
victims, 6

WEBSITES

Due to the changing nature of Internet links, PowerKids Press has developed an online list of websites related to the subject of this book. This site is updated regularly. Please use this link to access the list: www.powerkidslinks.com/chero/hstg